101

THINGS TO LOVE ABOUT

LAGUNA BEACH

Copyright © 2013
Brooks Street Books, Laguna Beach.

All rights reserved.

No part of this book may be
reproduced in any form without
written permission from the
publisher.

For information about
other titles by
Brooks Street Books, please see
www.brooksstreetbooks.com

Cover and interior designed
by Allison Hoffman-Tosti

Printed in China

ISBN 978-0-615-87051-9

101
THINGS TO LOVE ABOUT
LAGUNA BEACH

SALLY EASTWOOD & HELEN POLINS-JONES

FOR FIONA:
Always number one on my list
- Sally

FOR PHILLIP, BEN, OLIVIA, MONICA and LEN
- Helen

CONTENTS

PAGES 10-27 ....

PAGES 28-41 ....

PAGES 42-55 ....

PAGES 56-69 ....

PAGES 70-83 ....

PAGES 84-101 ....

PAGES 102-113 ....

PAGES 114-129 ....

PAGES 130-147 ....

PAGES 148-159 ....

- THE PAST
- OCEANS AND BEACHES
- COMMUNITY SPIRIT
- ART
- FOUR-LEGGED FRIENDS AND OTHER CREATURES
- NATURE, GARDENS AND FARMS
- PLACES TO EAT, DRINK, SHOP AND SLEEP
- ARCHITECTURE
- SPORTS ON LAND AND SEA
- FAMOUS PLACES AND FACES

INTRODUCTION

This book came into being through the love that two people have for their chosen hometown. When you wake up every day marveling at the beauty that surrounds you and basking in the sense of community that permeates Laguna Beach, it's hard not to shout it from the rooftops to anyone who'll listen. We realize that many people feel just the way we do, and decided to combine our talents to create something special, both for Laguna locals and all the visitors who come for a day, a week, or longer, who have also fallen in love with this unique town.

So, Sally tapped fingers to keyboard and Helen put paintbrush to paper, and what you're now holding in your hands is our own illustrated love letter to Laguna Beach.

The book isn't designed to be linear. You can flip to any page you like and read what's there. Or, pick a chapter that catches your attention and delve into it. Of course, you can just start at the beginning and read all the way to the end, and we hope you do — many times.

Before we begin, a few important notes. There are many wonderful books detailing Laguna Beach's beginnings, history and evolution, which we encourage you to seek out. This book is not intended to be a complete historical guide, but rather, to highlight a few of the more illuminating facts about Laguna's past. A list of sources referenced can be found in the appendix.

Also, like all communities, Laguna Beach continues to evolve: businesses and other establishments come and go, while natural elements (hopefully!) remain for a lifetime. For this reason we've not mentioned many places of business by name, but you will find a few, and we hope they're here for a long time. Maybe there will be 101 more reasons to write another book!

— Sally Eastwood & Helen Polins-Jones

THE PAST

OLD COAST HIGHWAY

1 THE FIRST HOMESTEADERS: 1870

Between 1870 and 1916, only thirty-one families lived in Laguna Beach. Prior to that, the region was home to the Juaneño Indians, the original inhabitants of the land that was to become Orange County. It was manpower from the Juaneño tribe that helped Father Juñipero Serra build California's seventh mission in San Juan Capistrano.

Back in the late 1800s, Los Angeles was a five-day journey away from Laguna Beach; San Diego, seven days. It was impossible to travel by horse-drawn wagon between Laguna and its neighbor to the south, Arch Beach, because the canyons were too deep. Access to town was via Laguna Canyon only.

So what's changed in 150 years? Well, not much. There are still only two ways in and out of Laguna Beach: Laguna Canyon Road and Pacific Coast Highway. As for the population, that's changed a little: almost 25,000 as of the last census.

The Wesley Thompson and Starkey families when they moved into Laguna Canyon.

who knew?

The Juaneño Indians named this area "Lagonas," their word for lake, after the two fresh water lagoons in Laguna Canyon.

FIRST RECORDED SUBDIVISION: 1887

In 1887, entrepreneur Henry Goff sold eleven fifty-foot wide, oceanfront lots to individual buyers. The price? Fifty bucks each: the deal of the century for sure. But not everyone was able to cash in on the boom. One early real estate investor, George Rogers, owned land in downtown Laguna Beach, but moved back to Missouri in 1893 when no one was interested in purchasing his subdivided lots for $10 each. Ouch! Despite the recent recession, houses and land in Laguna Beach continue to be among the most expensive in the country. Where's that time machine when you need it?

we love...

Three pre-1900 houses remain in Laguna Beach. The oldest is 154 Pearl Street, built in 1883.

LAGUNA PIERS: 1887 to 1970

Over a period of eighty-three years, four piers were constructed in Laguna Beach. The first was at Arch Beach, in 1887, used primarily to load hay onto ships bound for San Diego. Guests of the nearby Arch Beach Hotel also used the pier to fish or take a stroll. The second pier was built in 1896 off Heisler Park. The third, and longest, was completed in 1925, and measured 1,150 feet. The most recent pier was built in 1971 at Aliso Beach.

None of them remain today, having been destroyed or demolished over the decades. Now there's nothing to mar the sweeping ocean views, but then again, no place to admire the coastline from further out and observe marine life at play.

The old pier at HEISLER PARK

FIRST ART GALLERY: 1918

For almost a hundred years, Laguna has been known as a haven for artists of all types. The first art gallery was opened on Coast Highway next to what is now Hotel Laguna, and on the day it opened, over three hundred people came to view the works of twenty-two artists. Word spread, and within a month of opening, over two thousand people had visited the tiny space.

There are currently over fifty art galleries in town, offering a little something for everyone. They are a testament to the legacy of the Laguna Beach Art Association, founded in 1918, whose stated aim was "To advance the knowledge of, and interest in, Art, and to create a spirit of cooperation and fellowship between the painter and the public."

who knew?

The gallery built by the Laguna Beach Art Association in 1929 is now part of today's Laguna Art Museum.

PROHIBITION: 1920s ⑤

If you had to live through Prohibition, Laguna Beach was one of the places you could easily, albeit illegally, quench your thirst. Rumrunners in the 1920s brought liquor to the secluded beaches and coves of Laguna from Canada, transferring it to smaller boats, which were often painted black, to feign invisibility and avoid capture by the authorities.

Sometimes things didn't go exactly as planned. Legend has it that on one fateful evening, a boat ventured too close to the rocks, and its precious cargo of Scotch whiskey washed up on the sand, much to the delight of the locals. The news spread like wildfire, and there was a rush to grab as much bounty as possible. Ah, the good old days.

RUMRUNNER BOAT

THE GREETER: 1942

Danish-born Eiler Larsen, Laguna Beach's best-known official Greeter, arrived in 1942, thirty-four years after "Old Joe" Lucas, the first Greeter, died. Larsen was a self-proclaimed philosopher and lover of life. His usual greeting spot was the corner of Coast Highway and Forest Avenue, where he would stand and wave, offering small gifts and books to passersby. Larsen supported himself through gardening jobs and donations, and continued greeting until his health started to fail.

Larsen died in 1975, but his legacy and memory live on at the aptly-named Greeter's Corner Restaurant on Coast Highway next to Main Beach, where his footprints are cast in the sidewalk and his statue greets all who pass.

STATUE OF EILER LARSEN
AT THE OLD POTTERY PLACE

COUNTERCULTURE: 1960s

The times they were a'changin' all over the world in the 1960s, and Laguna was no exception. With a colorful history during the Prohibition era, it seems natural that Laguna Beach became the stomping grounds of the Brotherhood of Eternal Love and Timothy Leary in 1967. Dubbed "The Hippie Mafia," the Brotherhood produced and distributed drugs, hoping to start a psychedelic revolution in America.

Leary, who famously exhorted people to "turn on, tune in and drop out," was arrested regularly and held in twenty-nine different prisons throughout the world. One such incident occurred on Woodland Drive in Laguna Beach in 1968, when rookie police officer Neil Purcell, who later became Laguna's Chief of Police, arrested Leary for possession of marijuana.

The Brotherhood of Eternal Love disbanded in 1972 following multiple drug raids. Timothy Leary died in 1996, and a pinch of his ashes was sent into orbit on the same rocket that held *Star Trek* creator Gene Roddenberry's remains. A fitting way, perhaps, to gain the ultimate high.

who knew?

From December 25 through 27, 1970, the "Christmas Happening" was staged in Laguna Canyon. Dubbed "Woodstock West," the event was attended by roughly 25,000 revelers. A small plane swooped over the gathering, dropping thousands of Christmas cards, each containing a dose of Orange Sunshine, the Brotherhood of Eternal Love's brand of LSD. Some say that every scrap of paper was eaten and the canyon had never been so litter-free.

OLYMPIC VILLAGE: 1932

One year before the end of Prohibition, Los Angeles hosted the 1932 Olympic Games. Small two-room cottages were constructed close to the stadium to house the athletes during the two weeks of competition: the very first Olympic Village.

Once the games were over, a Laguna resident who owned land in Bluebird Canyon relocated many of the cottages to town. Check out the street names in upper Bluebird Canyon and you'll spot some US Olympians. Madison, Didrickson, Dyer, Metcalf, Wykoff, Crabbe and Jefferson were all athletes. Now their names live on in a small enclave of Laguna Beach.

THE FIRES: 1993

On October 27, 1993, Laguna Beach made headlines for all the wrong reasons. Thirteen separate blazes devastated southern California that day, and firefighting equipment was brought in from as far afield as San Francisco. Luckily, no one died, but the high number of homes lost was because the firefighters literally ran out of water. The city had been asking for additional reservoir resources, but it wasn't until after the fire that this came to fruition.

In the years since, Laguna has suffered other natural disasters: severe flooding and mudslides at Main Beach and the canyon in 1997, a major landslide in Bluebird Canyon in 2005, and yet more flooding in 2010 that smothered parts of Coast Highway with several feet of mud. Throughout all this, the spirit of Laguna never flags. The community pulls together, rebuilding commences and life goes on.

who knew?

The 1993 fires destroyed over 300 homes in Laguna Beach.

LAGUNA'S "WINDOW TO THE SEA:" 1968

You see it immediately when you drive down Broadway towards Coast Highway: the ocean, stretching out in front of you. So what? It's a seaside town; of course you can see the ocean. But Laguna Beach is one of very few oceanfront towns that have preserved their views against high-rises and hotels.

In 1968, the City of Laguna Beach purchased 1,000 feet of Main Beach ocean frontage, using bonds, to create a public park. It was agreed that the park would not be commercialized. Some developers had different ideas, including one plan for a five-story convention center. Thankfully, there was strong opposition from city residents, and Laguna was rewarded in 1975 with the Orange County Beautification Award for the park and the tree-planting program. So, go ahead and gaze at that view. It truly is one-of-a-kind.

OCEANS AND BEACHES

CRESCENT BAY

HOW MANY BEACHES?

The name Laguna Beach is a little misleading. You'd be forgiven for thinking that there's only one beach in town. In reality, there are over twenty-five beaches and coves in Laguna, from Crystal Cove in the north to Thousand Steps in the south. Everyone has a favorite. Do you prefer the open expanse and bustle of Main Beach? Or perhaps the diving opportunities at Shaw's Cove? Maybe surfing at one of the "street beaches" is more your style?

For the record, here's a list of the public beaches in Laguna. Take a weekend and visit them all.

Crystal Cove ☐
Crescent Bay ☐
Shaw's Cove ☐
Diver's Cove ☐
Picnic Beach ☐
Rockpile ☐
Main Beach ☐
Sleepy Hollow ☐
Cleo ☐
St. Ann's ☐
Thalia ☐
Anita ☐
Oak ☐
Brooks ☐ } street beaches
Cress ☐
Mountain ☐
Bluebird ☐
Agate ☐
Pearl ☐
Wood's Cove ☐
Moss Cove ☐
Victoria ☐
Treasure Island ☐
Aliso Beach ☐
Camel Point ☐
West Street ☐
Table Rock ☐
Thousand Steps ☐

WHALES

The sight of a whale up close, or even at a distance, can only be described as breathtaking. These huge, majestic mammals slowly wend their way up and down the Pacific Coast, providing opportunities to observe them from the shore, or from a whale-watching boat.

From November through May, gray whales migrate. Between April and November it's blue whales. There are also lesser-known species: fin and minke whales, so you're likely to spot something all year round. Southern California has more blue whales per square mile than anywhere else in the world. They are beneficiaries of the increased quantity of marine life. It's good to know there's plenty of plankton to fill those huge bellies as they commute up and down the coastline.

who knew?

Gray whales migrate around 15,000 miles or more per year, the longest migration of any mammal on earth.

ZERO TRASH 13

Have you ever noticed how clean the streets and beaches are in Laguna? Have you ever wondered why? It's thanks in large part to the initiative started by Zero Trash Laguna. This is a community project committed to clearing up waste, supporting local business and fostering a sense of environmental responsibility.

Zero Trash Laguna was founded in 2007, and on the first Saturday of each month, all are invited to a community cleanup event from 10 a.m. until noon. Armed with bags, gloves and T-shirts provided by local businesses, people young and old get involved to support this great cause. Over 60,000 pounds of trash, and counting, have been removed from Laguna's beaches since 2007.

we love...

The Zero Trash initiative is spreading to other cities in California and beyond.

SEA BIRDS

What is that little bird running back and forth with the waves? Sure, you'll recognize the seagulls as they cackle overhead and scavenge for scraps on the beach. You'll marvel at the elegant pelicans flying in their V-formation, swooping low to the water to grab a fish for breakfast. But there are other feathered friends to spot. From sandpipers and black oystercatchers to wandering tattlers and pelagic cormorants, Laguna is a shorebird's best friend too.

who knew?

Pelicans live for fifteen to twenty-five years in the wild, although one in captivity reached the age of fifty-four.

who's that bird?

WESTERN GULL

CURLEW

EGRET

15   KELP BEDS

You'll see them from afar as a dark mass in the ocean. If you're swimming or kayaking, you'll experience them up close and personal. Kelp beds are a very important indicator of the health of the ocean and are one of the most productive ecosystems on earth. With over eight hundred species relying on them, kelp forests are known as the rainforests of the sea. Just a few years ago, the kelp in the waters off Laguna's shoreline was diminishing, but a reforestation project initiated in 2002 by the California Coastkeeper Alliance has been very successful. Over twice as much kelp now exists in Laguna's waters as before the project began.

we love...

In conjunction with Earth Day each April, Laguna Beach holds an annual KelpFest to celebrate the return of the kelp forests. The festivities include educational displays about kelp and California marine life, live performances and, of course, food.

TIDE POOLS

Laguna Beach's rocky shoreline and numerous hidden coves provide many opportunities to view tide pools large and small. Tide pool "docents," volunteers trained by the Laguna Ocean Foundation, are available to educate the public about marine life and why tide pools are such an important part of the beach ecosystem.

Spend an hour or two at the beach below Heisler Park, Treasure Island, or one of many others, and see how many different species of flora and fauna you can spot. From sea anemones, hermit crabs and mussels to tiny shrimp and colorful sea stars, the variety is fascinating — and, fortunately for them and us, these creatures are protected by law. Laguna Beach is a designated Marine Protection Area as defined by the California Department of Fish and Game, meaning it's illegal to take anything from the ocean or the beach here — including the tide pools.

SEASHELLS AND SEAGLASS AND SEAWEED, OH MY!

Speaking of protection and preservation, you'll see many inanimate objects during your stroll along the beach. Like the living creatures, they too are protected under the Marine Life Protection Act. We all remember the days as kids when we wandered along the beach on our vacations, picking up a perfect shell to take home as a souvenir. Nowadays, it's better to leave those shells, and the seaglass and the seaweed and whatever else the tide has brought in, right there in the sand. Admire nature, preserve the beauty and live by the mantra: "Take only photographs, leave only footprints."

18

DOLPHINS

who knew?

Dolphins are the only mammals whose young are born tail-first instead of head-first.

Look carefully. What do you see out there in the ocean? Is that just a breaking wave or is it a fin? It's common to see dolphins frolicking in the ocean off the beaches in Laguna. Curious creatures, they follow paddle boarders and surfers, playing chase and chattering excitedly. They seem to know that these strange people in the water won't hurt them. We humans are entranced by these wonderful sea mammals, and it's likely that the dolphins are just as fascinated by us.

SEALS AND SEA LIONS

Seal Rock is the best place to find them, and if you're kayaking or paddle boarding, you can see them up close. Can you spot the different species?

California sea lions are smooth and sleek, about five to seven feet long. Northern elephant seals have elongated droopy noses and can grow up to ten feet long. Northern fur seals are, as the name suggests, furry with a shorter snout, between five and seven feet long. Finally, there are harbor seals. Stockier than the California sea lions, they are lighter in color, with shorter snouts and front flippers. Enjoy watching them play on the rocks. You'll be amazed how many can fit onto one tiny piece of real estate.

who knew?

Sea lions are sometimes called sea dogs because of the barking noise they make. Seals tend to make quieter grunting noises.

COMMUNITY SPIRIT

TRANSITION LAGUNA

In 2008 Laguna Beach became the tenth official "Transition Town" in the U.S., and there are currently 140 such towns in the country. So what is the Transition movement? Each Transition Town engages its residents at the grassroots level, striving to produce local food, water and energy, and to handle waste responsibly. Transition Laguna members sell vegetable and herb seedlings at the local farmers' market and hold workshops to educate the public on topics such as green building and gray-water usage.

who knew?

Laguna Beach currently receives all its water from as far away as the Colorado and Sacramento rivers. There is only a seven to ten day supply of water on hand in case of emergency.

Local, sustainable initiatives are the priority, such as planting edible gardens and sponsoring a food co-op each month, where people can drop off produce from their own plots and receive produce from others. So don't be surprised if you see gardens in Laguna Beach that look good enough to eat — they probably are.

FARMERS' MARKET

For over ten years, Laguna has held its farmers' market downtown next to City Hall every Saturday morning. It's small, but packed with local vendors who sell everything from organic produce to coffee, cheeses to chili, orchids to Afghan breads. Sip a freshly squeezed juice as you stroll around the stalls, and don't forget to check out the seedlings from Transition Laguna.

Laguna Beach has a public transportation system that's rare among cities its size. For less than a dollar, you can leave the car at home and board one of the blue city buses to get where you want to go. You may see things you never noticed from behind the wheel. There are three main lines: the Grey Route for Top of The World, Laguna Canyon and North Laguna; the Blue Route for Arch Beach Heights and Bluebird Canyon; and the Red Route for downtown to the Ritz Carlton, along Coast Highway.

In summer, there's something even better. Seven days a week, free trolleys traverse the coastline from Shaw's Cove in the north to Mission Hospital in the south, and up Laguna Canyon road to the festivals. Enjoy all the sights of town, with stops at convenient spots along the way. The service runs from 9:30 a.m. to 11:30 p.m. so it's also perfect for heading out to dinner when the day is done.

SUMMER TROLLEYS AND CITY BUSES

we love...

There's a "trolley tracker" on the free Laguna Beach Travel app so you can check when the next one will come along.

23 THE CRIME BLOTTER

Not many town newspapers detail such entertaining crimes as those in Laguna Beach. For locals, the crime blotter is a weekly must-read. Not that we're extolling the virtues of lawlessness; it's just that there are certain misdemeanors that make you smile.

For example, where else could you read about police responding to a report of "a neurologically impaired rat on the deck," or that "a woman claimed a man threw ice cream at her after she refused to go out with him." How about a pelican that "refused to leave the pool area for three days," or "a man stealing a block of cheese and hiding it in the bushes."

we love...

You can purchase "coaster crime" beverage coasters from some of Laguna's boutiques, where the strangest and funniest crime blotter entries have been captured for posterity.

PATRIOTS' DAY PARADE

Every year on the first Saturday in March, the town congregates to watch the annual Patriots' Day Parade. With close to a hundred floats, marching bands and vintage cars, it's said that half the town participates and the other half watches. For almost fifty years, the parade has brought people together with a theme that changes each year, but always celebrates love of country and love of community.

Organized and run by volunteers, the parade also honors local citizens. It's a great tradition that's become part of the fabric of Laguna Beach life.

RADIO STATION

It's tough to access radio stations in Laguna Beach. High canyon walls thwart even the strongest of signals; for over twenty years, the nearest and clearest FM radio stations were in Los Angeles and San Diego.

In 2012, that all changed. Laguna Beach now has its very own independent, community-supported radio station, KX 93.5 FM. Finally, a radio station you can hear — well, as long as you don't live south of the Montage, or north of Crystal Cove. But even if you can't listen on the airwaves, you can stream the station through your computer or smart phone. With shows hosted by Laguna residents and a generational alt-rock format, KX 93.5 will remind you of your favorite college station. You can hear live, in-studio performances by local bands, and get up-to-the-minute surf reports.

who knew?

From 1949 to 1951, Laguna Beach had an AM radio station: KTED.

26

HALLOWEEN ON OAK STREET

Who doesn't love Halloween? Not just the candy, but also the costumes, the decorations and the parties. There are many great places to go trick-or-treating in Laguna, and kid-friendly events to attend, like Boo Blast at El Morro School. But the granddaddy of them all is Oak Street. Oak and Brooks Streets are cordoned off to cars each year, enabling pedestrians to wander freely, collecting candy and marveling at the ghoulish décor. If you drive by the day before Halloween, you'd never know anything was going to happen. Then, on October 31, there's a frenzy of activity as residents decorate and prepare for the deluge of visitors. From twilight to around ten in the evening, hundreds of people gather in the streets and a wickedly good time is had by all. Well, that is until the next day, when there's all that cleaning up to do.

HOSPITALITY NIGHT

On the first Friday in December, the holiday spirit arrives in Laguna, along with Santa Claus himself. Hospitality Night is the official start of the season, and lower Forest Avenue is closed to traffic for the occasion. The eucalyptus trees lining the street are wrapped with lights, the pepper tree outside City Hall is lit for all to see, and Santa and Mrs. Claus arrive in style on one of the city's fire trucks. This is a true community gathering. Shops and restaurants offer mulled wine and snacks, music plays, choirs sing and bagpipers parade. For many locals — especially children seeing Santa for the first time — it's the most special night of the year.

we love...

Laguna Beach's movie theater screens *It's a Wonderful Life* every Hospitality Night.

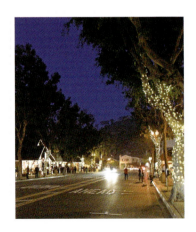

MUSIC IN THE PARK

During the summer, what could be better than heading to a local park on a Sunday afternoon, spreading a blanket on the grass, opening a picnic basket of goodies and reclining with a glass of lemonade (or something stronger) — all while enjoying live music? And did we mention this is free?

On Sunday afternoons from late July to late August, Bluebird Park plays host to bands of all types, from reggae to rock, and the community gathers to eat and drink, dance and play. All ages are welcome — just make sure you get there early enough to stake your place on the grass. By about 5 p.m. when it all begins, the lawn is a patchwork quilt of blankets, and friends old and new, kids and parents, and even some grandparents, are alternately relaxing on the grass and dancing up a storm.

PARKING METERS FOR THE HOMELESS

Have you ever wondered about those brightly painted meters that look more like works of art than utilitarian metal poles? Here's a hint: they're not positioned by the side of the road. Rather, they're at the intersections of Laguna's busy downtown streets: Forest Avenue and Glenneyre; Coast Highway and Laguna Avenue; Coast Highway and Ocean Avenue; and Ocean Avenue and Broadway. Painted by local artists, these meters collect quarters that are donated to the city to provide resources for the homeless and help to prevent panhandling. A decorative way to raise money for a good cause.

who knew?

The Alternative Sleeping Location for the homeless opened on Laguna Canyon Road in 2010.

30

RELIGIOUS DIVERSITY

For such a small city, Laguna Beach offers a wide variety of places to worship. You'll find churches dedicated to these faiths, in no particular order: Presbyterian, Catholic, Unitarian, Jewish, Mormon, Hare Krishna, Episcopal, Christian Science, Evangelical, Methodist, Jehovah's Witness, American Catholic and probably a few more.

When December comes around, there's something uniquely Laguna that appears on Main Beach for the eight days of Hanukkah: a surfboard menorah, featuring donated surfboards. The lighting ceremony is accompanied each year by live music, dancing and crafts for the kids. No matter what your faith, it's fun for everyone.

ART

HEISLER PARK

31 FESTIVAL OF ARTS

The Festival of Arts began in 1932 as a small show. Its organizers, the Laguna Beach Art Association, hoped to draw some additional business to town once the Los Angeles Olympics concluded. Over eighty years on, the Festival is now one of the nation's oldest and most highly acclaimed juried art shows. One hundred and forty of Orange County's finest artists exhibit paintings, sculpture, photography, jewelry, ceramics, furniture and more. In addition to art, the festival grounds play host to live music, demonstrations, art workshops and special events, making the venue a must-see all summer long.

who knew?

The Junior Art Exhibit at the Festival started in 1947, and each year showcases over three hundred works of art by Orange County students, from kindergarten through twelfth grade.

LAGUNA ART MUSEUM

Prominently located on Coast Highway, the Laguna Art Museum is unique among all other museums in the state. It collects and displays only California art, either created by artists living in California, or portraying the history of the state itself. Tracing its origins back to the original Laguna Beach Arts Association founded in 1918, the museum's permanent collection consists of over 3,500 works of art from the nineteenth century to the present day.

Revolving exhibitions run the gamut. Examples include glamour photography of the 1920s and '30s, a retrospective of Japanese American designer Osamu Noguchi, and "Art Shack," thirty different worlds constructed within the museum, blurring the lines between art and architecture. The gift shop is a great resource for locals and tourists alike, with books, postcards, ceramics and more.

ART BENCH OUTSIDE
THE LAGUNA ART MUSEUM

who knew?

In 1957, Bette Davis was scheduled to appear in the Pageant for one night, but had to drop out due to a last-minute injury. However, her rehearsal photos garnered a lot of press for the Pageant!

PAGEANT OF THE MASTERS

Staged in the Irvine Bowl amphitheater on the Festival of Arts grounds, the Pageant of the Masters is one of the most unique productions in the world, providing the illusion of "tableaux vivants," or living pictures. Each year, a specific theme is chosen, and, for ninety minutes every night during the summer season, the stage is set. Hundreds of volunteers in costume pose as the characters within well-known paintings and sculptures, accompanied by an orchestra and expert narration. With the trick of stage lighting, three-dimensional figures are magically transformed into two-dimensional canvases: it really is tough to tell where the backdrop ends and the human bodies begin.

Since 1933 this amazing spectacle has entranced audiences, especially during the popular "build" sequences, where the back-stage machinations to bring the pictures to life are shown to the crowd. By tradition, no matter what the year's theme is, the final picture of the evening is always Leonardo da Vinci's *The Last Supper*, providing a spectacular finale.

SAWDUST FESTIVAL

Tucked away along Laguna Canyon Road, the Sawdust Festival offers handmade treasures in a rustic setting that is literally sprinkled with sawdust underfoot. From jewelry to pottery, paintings to clothing, you'll find a special something for people on your list, or, for yourself. Linger for the glass-blowing demonstrations and the live music. In summer, it's sublime; in winter, truly magical. Stroll amidst a flurry of snowflakes while a Dickensian chorus sings Christmas carols, or visit Santa in his home away from home and buy one-of-a-kind ornaments for the tree. Sawdust memories will last a lifetime.

ART-A-FAIR

The Art-A-Fair venue sits close to the Sawdust Festival grounds on Laguna Canyon Road. Like the other summer festivals, Art-A-Fair bustles for two months of the year, visited by both locals and tourists. Unlike the other summer festivals, Art-A-Fair isn't only for Orange County artists; over 125 artists from across the country and around the world showcase two- and three-dimensional pieces. With an acclaimed restaurant on site and live entertainment on the weekends, you can stroll around to see your favorite pieces and even watch the artists work in a quiet garden setting.

we love...

During Art Walk, the free trolley shuttle runs from Jasmine Street in North Laguna to Bluebird Canyon Drive, so you can get around town with ease.

FIRST THURSDAYS ART WALK

The name says it all. On the first Thursday of every month, the galleries in town stay open from 6 to 9 p.m., and welcome the public to meander, socialize and view art pieces. Hors d'oeuvres and wine are available at most establishments. It's become customary for other stores along Coast Highway and the surrounding streets to remain open and hold their own events during Art Walk, meaning you can find a plethora of interesting things to do during the evening, as well as eat and drink, of course.

LAGUNA PLAYHOUSE

Founded in 1920, the Laguna Playhouse is the oldest continuously operating theater company on the west coast. The original playhouse artists performed in private houses and stores until its first official home was built in 1924 on Ocean Avenue. As the productions grew in scope and size, audiences also grew, and in 1969, the playhouse's current home was constructed on Laguna Canyon Road, providing a larger venue with better equipment.

In 1996, the Laguna Playhouse became a professional non-profit theater. Since that time, its reputation has steadily grown and it's recognized nationally for the quality of its productions. Today, more than one hundred thousand patrons each season attend performances ranging from comedy, drama, musical theater and youth productions. Almost a hundred years on, the Laguna Playhouse continues to thrive.

who knew?

Harrison Ford is a distinguished alumnus of the Laguna Playhouse.

ART IN PUBLIC PLACES

You don't need to enter a gallery to spot art in Laguna Beach. Many stunning examples can be spotted on the streets too. The Art in Public Places project is funded by both the city and private developers. There are mosaics at The Old Pottery Place, a turquoise porcelain wall sculpture at The Montage, a colorful giant tortoise in Bluebird Park and poetic railings at Brown's Park on Coast Highway. Artist Benches are also part of this program and you'll find creative and practical examples all around Laguna, including a bench perched on geometric shapes outside the Art Museum.

To see where all the public art pieces are located, check out the map on the city's website, which includes photos, descriptions and quotes by the artists. Every year, the list grows, so there's always something new to see.

"THE SHOPPER"
BY ANDREW MYERS

LAGUNA COLLEGE OF ART AND DESIGN

Founded in 1961 as the Laguna Beach School of Art, Laguna College of Art and Design now offers degrees in Animation, Graphic Design and Game Art, as well as Bachelor's and Master's degrees in Fine Art. The nine-acre campus is nestled on Laguna Canyon Road, surrounded by trees and large sculptural pieces. With a student body of only four hundred, the competition to gain entry is fierce.

we love...

Students from LCAD designed and painted the mural "Wonder" on one of the walls of Laguna Canyon Winery.

PLEIN AIR PAINTING

One of Laguna Beach's signature events is the Plein Air Painting Invitational. This weeklong landscape painting festival, held each October, attracts oil, pastel and watercolor artists from near and far, who set up their easels along the coastline and paint what they see. The public is invited to stroll around, watching as each canvas evolves from an outline sketch to a finished masterpiece.

who knew?

The Laguna Beach Plein Air Painters' Association (LPAPA) was founded in 1996 by five Laguna Beach artists to renew interest in outdoor landscape painting.

At the conclusion of the festival, the works of art are framed and displayed at a public art show and sale. What better souvenir of Laguna is there than a piece of art you see being created before your eyes?

FOUR-LEGGED FRIENDS

AND OTHER CREATURES

PACIFIC MARINE MAMMAL CENTER

THE DOG PARK

On Laguna Canyon Road, a small slice of freedom for dogs and their owners beckons. Between dawn and dusk every clear day (except Wednesdays), off-leash dogs can run and sniff to their hearts' content, chasing balls, playing tag and generally working off steam. A large grassy area, fresh water and doggie bags aplenty make this a great spot to hang for both dogs and people. If your pooch is petite, there's a separate area to frolic, but don't be surprised if she wants to run with the big dogs.

who knew?

The Laguna Beach Dog Park opened in 1992 and was the first dog park in Orange County.

PACIFIC MARINE MAMMAL CENTER

Housed in a red barn on Laguna Canyon Road, with a design more New England than Southern California, the Pacific Marine Mammal Center is a haven for sick and injured pinnipeds. The staff and volunteers rescue and rehabilitate seals and sea lions stranded along the Orange County shore, releasing them back to the wild when they're healthy and strong. Human contact is kept to a minimum to ensure that the sociable sea lions don't bond with their human helpers. That way, when it's time to say hello to the ocean again, they gambol happily home.

Releases are scheduled regularly at a few of Laguna's beaches. So if you get the chance, head down to watch in awe as a creature of the wild makes its way back to the ocean.

we love...

You can sponsor a seal or sea lion through the Pacific Marine Mammal Center, and you'll be notified when it's ready to be released.

LAGUNA BEACH ANIMAL SHELTER

Started in 1975 by a group of volunteers, the animal shelter is now funded by the city and through donations. As a small community, Laguna Beach is fortunate: eighty percent of animals arriving at the shelter are reunited with their owners within a few days. Animals include cats, dogs, birds, rabbits and other small animals — all available for adoption once they're cleared medically. The adoption process is detailed and fastidious, to ensure that each animal is placed in the best possible home for its needs.

If you're looking to add a furry friend to your family, wherever you live, please visit your local animal shelter first. The perfect pet is probably there waiting for you.

who knew?

The Laguna Beach Animal Shelter has a return rate of only five percent, compared to the national average shelter attrition rate of fifty percent.

BLUE BELL FOUNDATION FOR CATS

Where do lucky cats go when they retire? Laguna Beach, of course. The Blue Bell Country Club for Cats started off in the 1960s as a temporary boarding facility. Over time, the owner of the property started taking in strays and cats whose owners could no longer take care of them.

The Blue Bell Foundation was created in 1989 and now houses around fifty felines on two acres of land in the canyon. The cats live in a cage-free environment where they can snooze and play, cared for by volunteer staff and skilled veterinarians. Supported by donations and placement fees, the foundation does have some cats available for adoption; however, many live out their remaining years at the facility. Now that's a retirement home.

GOATS:
THE FOUR-LEGGED FIREFIGHTERS

Just how do you keep the steep Laguna Beach hillsides safe from the threat of wildfires when it's impossible to mow those brushy slopes? You hire a team that's willing and able to access all terrain and clear every single piece of scrub, all year round, without pay. Meet Laguna Beach's four-legged firefighters. Around six hundred goats patrol over 640 acres of hillside, chomping on coastal sage scrub, chaparral and mustard, clearing the firebreaks and protecting homes. Heralded by FEMA (the Federal Emergency Management Agency) as a best practice in vegetation management, the program has been in place since 1995, providing a picturesque scene as the goats make their way around the city.

So if you're driving around and spot some dots up on a hillside, take another look: you've probably found the goats.

who knew?

The original name for Glenneyre Street was "Goat Trail."

DOG-FRIENDLY RESTAURANTS AND HOTELS

There are almost as many dogs in Laguna Beach as there are people, so it only makes sense that there are dining establishments in town that have dog-friendly patio areas so people can enjoy a cup of coffee or a meal with their four-legged friend by their side. If you're walking around town, you can take your dog into some Laguna stores and boutiques, where a tasty snack may also be offered. Everyone in Laguna, it seems, loves dogs.

Many Laguna hotels also offer pet-friendly rooms. From cozy bed and breakfasts to luxurious resorts, you'll find accommodations in every price range. Some have a weight maximum (for your dog, not you) so it's best to check ahead to be sure.

we love...

Over thirty dining establishments in town allow dogs on the premises, so you're bound to find a place to suit both you and your pooch.

COYOTES

who knew?

The name "coyote" is derived from the Aztec word "coyotl," meaning "trickster."

Laguna's canyons teem with wildlife of every kind. If you live close to the wilderness area, you're likely to see some of the indigenous residents on a regular basis. Coyotes used to be a rare sighting, but now they range closer to civilization, and it's not uncommon to be walking on a trail and spot one or more of them. As beautiful as they are, they can be dangerous. Laguna Beach residents are careful to keep cats and small dogs indoors as much as possible. If you see a sign saying "Lost Cat," unfortunately, it's likely to have been eaten.

So, respect the wilderness area and the coyotes. Don't tempt them closer to residences, and acknowledge that as beautiful as they are, they're also predators.

WILD ANIMALS

You'll spot creatures great and small in the canyons of Laguna Beach. Squirrels and bunnies abound. They love to congregate early in the morning on dew-laden grass, scampering away when approached. Roadrunners and lizards hustle down the trails on their way to very important business. You may even see a tarantula, although those sightings are rare.

Watch out for the rattlesnakes. The hotter the day, the more likely they are to be out basking in the sun and to cross your path. Keep dogs leashed, and try to avoid small holes in the trail and tall grasses. Rattlesnake bites can be fatal.

who knew?

Baby rattlesnakes are more dangerous than adult snakes since they emit all their venom when they bite: they don't know when to stop.

㊾ BOBCATS

Bobcats also roam the Laguna Beach wilderness. Majestic, with markings similar to those of a leopard or tiger, these cats can reach thirty-five pounds or more, and can be deadly to unprotected small animals. You may see one or two on the trails and most of the time, they'll run away when approached by humans. Take a picture if you can; otherwise just keep on walking. The wilderness is big enough for all of us.

we love...

Baby bobcats are called "kits."

BIRDS

When it comes to feathered friends, Laguna plays host to raptors of all sizes, from ospreys and falcons to hawks and even eagles. You'll see them hunting rodents in the wilderness, gliding high, then swooping low for the catch. On a smaller scale, you may hear the buzzing of tiny wings, and high-pitched tweeting: hummingbirds. It's great fun to put out a bottle or two of nectar and watch a throng of the tiny birds stop to drink. The moments before sunset appear to be "flappy hour" for hummingbirds, a popular drinking time. See how close you can get: hummingbirds are relatively comfortable around humans, and you may even catch a glimpse of their tiny tongues, lapping up the liquid.

we love...

Hummingbirds almost always lay two white eggs, each the size of a jellybean.

NATURE, GARDENS AND FARMS

CANYON ACRES TRAIL

51

PARKS

Laguna Beach has a plethora of parks dotted along the coast and further inland. For a beachside stroll, Heisler Park has incredible coastline views. Bluebird Park is great for kids (don't miss the giant mosaic tortoise). Moulton Meadows offers lighted tennis courts, a basketball court, a playground and soccer field, all on the edge of the wilderness.

And don't forget the "pocket parks," tiny parcels carved out to provide a quiet, green place to sit and admire the view. Brown's Park on Coast Highway, Nita Carman Park by the high school, and Arch Beach Heights view park all offer quiet slices of calm in which to watch the world go by.

MEDITERRANEAN CLIMATE

Laguna Beach is blessed with one of the most ideal climates in the world: the Mediterranean climate. This is what gives us warm summers with very little humidity, mild winters that encourage the growth of winter plants, and enough rain to keep the hillsides green. There are only five regions of the world that enjoy the same climate, and they're all positioned at the western edges of continents.

In the northern hemisphere, there's the Mediterranean area itself, encompassing southern Europe and parts of northern Africa, plus the southern California coastline. In the southern hemisphere there's the coastal area of central Chile, the western cape of South Africa, and the coastline of south and southwest Australia.

For residents, this is one of the greatest reasons to live here. It's rarely too hot or too cold to go out for a run on the beach or a hike in the hills, which means everyone spends a lot of time outdoors. For visitors, any time of the year is a good time to come to Laguna. And you don't need bug spray!

MOUNTAINS

Laguna is bordered to the west by the Pacific Ocean and to the east by the Santa Ana Mountains that separate Orange County from Riverside County. The two highest peaks, Modjeska at 5,496 feet and Santiago at 5,689 feet, together form the distinctive Saddleback Ridge, which you can easily see from the hillside walking trails in Laguna Beach. In wintertime, Saddleback is occasionally dusted with snow, and on a clear day it looks as close as Catalina Island to the west.

It's this stunning topography that makes the view of the mountains as compelling as that of the ocean, and for those who can see both — as is the case with many of Laguna's hillside residents — it's truly the best of both worlds.

54

HIKING TRAILS

Of course it's the ocean that draws people to Laguna Beach, but if you prefer your outdoor action on land, there's plenty of that too. There are many trails in Laguna, and you'll soon find your favorite for walking, jogging, hiking or mountain biking. From gently undulating paths to steep mountain trails, there's something for all experience levels.

If you hike these trails with your dog, you'll meet other walkers on quiet mornings when the dew rests upon the spider webs, creating jeweled ornaments hanging among the bushes and grass. It's moments like that when you can really feel at one with nature.

we love...

The Laguna Canyon Foundation offers guided hikes in the wilderness parks that include walking for fitness, bird watching, and finding edible and useful plants.

55

HORTENSE MILLER GARDEN

In North Laguna there's a hidden, two and a half acre garden that's open to the public. It showcases the wide range of plants that can be grown in the southern California coastal zone, all maintained with minimal use of chemical fertilizers to ensure diversity and to inspire people to see what they can do in their own gardens.

Hortense Miller was a native of St. Louis, Missouri who had an interest in all things botanical. She graduated from college in 1930 during the Great Depression and, unable to find a teaching job, taught herself to draw by copying illustrations in books. However, what she really wanted was a garden. Hortense and her husband, Oscar moved to Laguna Beach in 1958 when she was about to turn fifty, searching for a place to build her dream garden. And build it she did. She gave the City of Laguna Beach title to her property in the 1970s on the condition that it remain cultivated, open to the public, and not built upon. Her legacy remains, as The Friends of The Hortense Miller Garden raise money for upkeep and volunteer docents escort visitors around this slice of botanical paradise.

ALOE IN BLOOM

who knew?

Hortense Miller lived and worked on the garden for almost half a century, until her death in 2008, just six weeks short of her hundredth birthday.

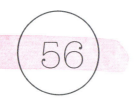

ORCHARDS, VINEYARDS AND FARMS

Nestled into the hillsides of Laguna Beach are a number of small agricultural enterprises that make the most of the Mediterranean climate, growing produce of all types and even grapes for wine. Fruit trees in residential back yards are common, with lemons, limes, grapefruit, figs and avocados being some of the most popular.

You'll also spot vegetable patches in gardens. They all yield produce for individual and family consumption, and there are more smallholdings popping up each day. Lagunans embrace growing their own food — the freshest you can possibly get.

who knew?

Figs have been used as a coffee substitute and, due to their high alkalinity, are eaten as an aid by those who wish to quit smoking.

WATER DISTRICT WATER-WISE GARDEN

Why would a garden belonging to a city office be part of this book? Well, the folks at the Laguna Beach County Water District really practice what they preach, and have set a tangible example for the community by planting a water-friendly garden right on their doorstep. Established in 2003, the garden shows that landscaping can be water-efficient, fire-safe and beautiful. The garden is also equipped with a weather-based "smart timer" controller that automatically adjusts based on the season, climate and weather conditions. Now that's efficient.

we love...

There are over fifty different types of plants, shrubs and perennials, along with photos and descriptions, that visitors can peruse as they stroll through the Water District's water-wise garden.

SOUTH LAGUNA COMMUNITY GARDEN

In 2009, a weedy vacant lot on Coast Highway at Eagle Rock Way was transformed into the South Laguna Community Garden. The land was donated and garden members volunteer in the construction and ongoing maintenance of beds and plantings.

The aim of the project is to provide fruit, vegetables and flowers for member families and friends of the garden, and to teach sustainable cultivation techniques. There's no doubt that the sense of camaraderie created by this enterprise has brought people together in a way that's a throwback to an earlier era. No matter what the future holds, the commitment to keeping a community garden is strong, so there will be a communal plot somewhere in South Laguna that will continue to thrive.

LAGUNA COAST WILDERNESS PARK

Areas of the Wilderness Park, located in Laguna Canyon, contain rocks that date back sixty-five million years to the time when dinosaurs roamed the earth. You can also find scallop fossils from twenty-five million years ago, when salt water covered the park and sea creatures thrived. Ten million-year-old giant shark teeth were discovered when the rocks were carved to create the road passing through, and human habitation of the canyon dates back to 2000 B.C.

Many centuries later, the citizens of Laguna Beach marched together in 1989 to protect this land from development, creating a protected greenbelt area, and in 1993, the Laguna Beach Wilderness Park opened. Today, tens of thousands of visitors enjoy the park every year, traversing more than forty miles of trails. In 2007, the Nix Nature Center opened its doors, educating the public about the geological past, as well as native flora and fauna. Take a hike and enjoy the scenery. It'll be here for millions of years to come.

who knew?

One species of plant, *Dudleya stolonifera*, commonly known as "Laguna Beach liveforever," is found nowhere else in the world except Laguna Canyon. It's so rare that it's federally listed as a threatened species.

FLOWERS FOR ALL SEASONS

Traditionally it's spring when wildflowers start to bloom, the promise of warmer days ahead. Spring flowers abound in Laguna Beach, with April being the most abundant month. A walk along any path will yield the joys of wild hyacinth, lupine, poppies, mariposa lilies and more. You'll also spot striking birds of paradise and other exotics. The colors span the spectrum and delight the eye.

But it's wintertime when the surprises pop up. As most of the country's vegetation sleeps for the winter, Laguna's aloe plants sprout and bloom. Bright orange flowers spear the sky with succulent green leaves below. You'll see them along the coastline where the contrast against the bright blue ocean and sky is a striking reminder that winter is here.

JUNE GLOOM AND INDIAN SUMMERS

Summertime isn't actually the warmest time of the year in Laguna Beach. As summer vacations begin in June, the skies in Laguna are generally overcast. If you travel inland, you'll often find that the temperature is at least ten degrees higher and you can actually see the sun. The "June gloom" phenomenon is well documented, and seems to be occurring even earlier in the year — "May gray" is now just as ubiquitous.

The hottest time of the year often begins in September or even October, just as locals are gearing up for Halloween. The best part is that it's quiet. Kids are back in school, folks are back at work and the city basks in its Indian summer. Thanksgiving is beautifully warm, and Christmas on the beach isn't unusual at all. So if you're planning a visit from out of town and you'd like to see the quieter side of Laguna Beach with a guarantee of gorgeous weather, we'll see you in the fall.

who knew?

Some people think the mist hovering over the ocean and rising up the canyons is plain old fog, but it's actually produced by a phenomenon called a marine layer. This occurs in coastal areas when the cool air over the ocean meets the warmer mass of air above.

GLORIOUS SUNSETS

Laguna Beach is fortunate to play host to gorgeous sunsets that light up the sky most nights of the year. There's something mesmerizing about watching that ball of fire descend slowly into the ocean. And the displays of color are stunning. Deep reds, purples, oranges, ochers and yellows abound; and yes, you may even see that elusive green flash. The hotter the day, the more intense the sunset. With different cloud formations every day, Mother Nature paints a unique canvas every night and it never gets old.

PLACES TO
EAT, DRINK, SHOP AND SLEEP

HOTEL LAGUNA

RESTAURANTS

Laguna Beach is a town with about 25,000 year-round residents and hundreds of thousands of tourists who visit every year. Everyone needs to eat, right? There are dining options in every price range that feature a wide selection of global cuisines, including French, Caribbean, Greek, Indian, Italian, Japanese, Thai and even Belgian and South African fare, as well as California contemporary. Most eateries are clustered along Coast Highway, Forest Avenue and Glenneyre Street, with others in the canyon.

Take a five-minute stroll in any direction from the downtown area and you'll pass a multitude of restaurants. Take a drive further south and you'll find some smaller places off the beaten path that are equally yummy and less crowded. Bon appétit!

BARS

If you're looking for a spot to take a load off and linger over a beer or a cocktail, you'll find many places in Laguna Beach that offer a comfortable bar stool and live music if you want it. Some of these establishments have long and colorful histories. The White House on Coast Highway opened in 1918, and is one of the oldest bars and restaurants in Orange County. There are also many newer, sleeker drinking establishments in town. So whether you want to drink beer at a well-worn bar with a great story, or dress up and people watch while you sip your cocktail, you'll find an option that suits you in Laguna. Cheers!

who knew?

The White House was a popular spot with Hollywood stars. Bing Crosby once signed more than fifty autographs there in 1938.

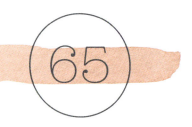

CAFES

For casual dining, whether breakfast or lunch, there are plenty of cafes to choose from in Laguna. Many have outdoor patio areas on which to people watch and linger with a latte. You'll find traditional breakfasts, specialty sandwiches and spectacular salads. Some specialize in vegetarian or vegan options and on sunny weekends it can be standing room only.

Every local has their favorite place and many visitors return to the same spots each year for a favorite dish. Bring a friend, bring a newspaper, bring your dog, and above all, bring a smile and enjoy the ambiance.

HOTELS 66

If the array of places to eat in Laguna is impressive, the variety of hotels in which to lay your head after a day of eating, shopping and beach hopping, is equally broad. From the ultimate in luxury to budget-conscious bargains, romantic and chic to sleek and modern, there's something to suit all tastes and price ranges.

And while it's true that these establishments cater primarily to visitors, they are also available all year round to locals who enjoy spa facilities with innovative treatments, great restaurants and beachfront walks.

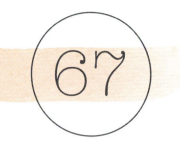

GUEST COTTAGES

As an alternative to hotels and motels, consider renting a cottage if you're visiting from out of town. Small and private, these offer a home away from home for individuals, couples or families, with kitchen facilities, so you have the choice to eat in as well as out. Within walking distance of all the beaches, cottages can provide a cost-effective option for accommodations. Out of season, these cottages are often vacant and their owners are looking for bookings. Prices drop and it's a great opportunity for locals to take a "staycation" in their own town. A getaway, without having to go away.

we love...

Actress Joan Crawford often stayed at the Yellow Cottage on Manzanita Street, with her fourth husband. She may even have spent her honeymoon there.

CAMPSITES

Camping in Laguna Beach? Yes, it's now possible. Just north of town, the El Moro State Park Campground opened in 2011, meaning you can spend a night in Laguna for around $50 per night — a bargain compared to other accommodation options.

The site is right next to Laguna Beach's El Morro Elementary School and opposite the upscale, gated community of Irvine Cove. Although spending the night in a tent isn't for everyone, the views are spectacular and the campground is new, fresh and clean. Be warned: the sites book up fast, so if this is something that interests you, plan ahead.

UNIQUE BOUTIQUES

Shopping is an art in Laguna Beach, literally as well as metaphorically. There are very few chain stores, no big-box retailers (not that there's anywhere to put them), and every establishment is unique. Clothing and accessories; skincare and perfumes; kitchenware, hardware and more can be found downtown and along Coast Highway.

Take a peek inside the beautifully decorated spaces for essentials and gifts. You'll occasionally find brands available nowhere in southern California except here in Laguna, or one-of-a-kind items you won't find anywhere else in the world.

CHEESE, CHOCOLATE, CUPCAKES AND COFFEE

The four food groups, right?

If you're craving something savory or sweet, or that special cup of joe, you've come to the right place. Artisan cheeses can be found in a couple of locations, as well as in a Laguna restaurant where a "Cheese Concierge" will make recommendations. Specialty chocolates can be purchased in stores that fill alleyways with aromatic cocoa scents. You'll find cupcakes for all seasons and all reasons, and last but not least, if caffeine is your dream, you can buy a pound of the finest coffee beans, sourced from around the world and roasted right here in Laguna Beach. Is your mouth watering yet?

we love...

Peppertree Lane is a European-style alleyway lined with stores and restaurants constructed around a pepper tree in 1934.

SPAS

How about heading somewhere you can eat, drink, shop AND sleep, almost simultaneously? You'll find both day spas and destination spas in town, where you can sip a selection of herbal teas, munch on fruits and nuts, buy those essential lotions, potions and relaxation aids, and, of course doze off on the massage table if you're so inclined.

Whether you choose the ambiance of a hotel spa, the convenience of a specialized day spa, or the serenity of a spa in the Canyon, there's a plethora of restorative treatments to be found in Laguna Beach.

we love...

Many spas incorporate fresh seasonal ingredients into treatments that are made daily for both your body and face — an innovative way to add more fruits and vegetables to your diet!

LAGUNA CANYON WINERY

If local-roasted coffee has you yearning for more, then how about Laguna Beach's very own wine? Laguna Canyon Winery opened in 2003, with a mission to create "Handcrafted California Wines." The grapes are plucked from small, low-yield vineyards in Napa Valley and Sonoma, transported to the winery in Laguna Beach, then crushed, pressed, fermented and bottled.

The winery holds tasting sessions and sells its wine not only on site, but also in fifteen other states. Whether you prefer red, white, pink or sparkling, there's something for every taste and it makes a great gift — for your friends and family, or your own personal cellar.

ARCHITECTURE

ST. FRANCIS-BY-THE-SEA CATHEDRAL

 # UPSIDE-DOWN HOUSES

Laguna Beach's incredible ocean views are appreciated by everyone, especially residents. If you have a house with a vista of the coastline and Catalina Island, you want to gaze at that view as much as possible when you're home. That means creating spaces with living areas upstairs to take advantage of the higher aspect, and bedrooms downstairs where they're more private and shaded. It's completely logical and many houses on the Laguna hillsides are built that way.

So, if you ever hear someone say that they head downstairs to bed and climb upstairs for breakfast, chances are they live in Laguna Beach, or a town very like it.

74

CLIFFHANGERS

Laguna Beach's topography ranges from relatively flat along the coastline and in the village, to rolling hills and canyon cliffs. Often compared to the French Riviera, Laguna does feel very much like Monte Carlo or Cannes when you're driving along the slopes of Alta Vista, Summit Drive or Temple Hills Drive.

When buildable lots consist of no flat land at all, constructing a home is an art and a challenge. These cliffhangers deceive the eye. If you pass by the front façade of many hillside homes, all you'll see is a garage door and what looks like a single level. It's around the back that the magic happens. Everything cascades down that hill — two, three or more levels. Again, it's all about the view. So don't write off what may look like a boring exterior. Once you step inside, it's a different world.

QUAINT COTTAGES

In the village area of Laguna Beach you'll find the earliest residences in the city. Between 1883 and 1940, many different styles of cottage were constructed, from craftsman and Cotswold to bungalows and beach cottages. Some remain just as they were years ago, and may even be owned by members of the same families that built them. Many have been carefully updated over the years, while remaining true to the original design.

Stroll around the quiet lanes and admire the variety of cottages and their beautiful gardens. In some areas it feels more English country than southern California, and that's yet another thing to love about Laguna Beach.

who knew?

Beach cottages often started as one room and were added onto over time. The original one-room weekend houses were "overlooked" for taxation purposes since they were not the main family home.

MODERN MANSIONS

In stark contrast to Laguna's cottages, you'll find many modern architectural masterpieces scattered around town. Whether oceanfront or perched on hills to take advantage of the views, many of these concrete and glass edifices feature cutting edge angles, sweeping decks and the blurring of boundaries between inside and out.

Equally impressive are the contemporary houses that draw on more traditional architectural styles. Cut stone, terracotta tiled roofs and warm Mediterranean hues adorn many homes in the area, bringing a southern European influence to southern California. Light, airy and spacious, these homes epitomize what breezy coastal living is all about.

we love...

Laguna Beach is home to some very talented architects, who are responsible for many of the modern masterpieces in town.

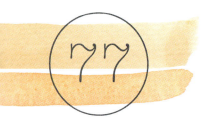

ECLECTIC ABODES

There are a few houses in Laguna Beach that are so unique that they are well known and often photographed. The "Witch's House" on Wave Street is one of them. Built over a period of five years from 1924 to 1929 by architect Vernon Barker on his weekends, this home really does look like it belongs in a fairy tale. With its steep gables and strange angles, there's not a straight line in sight.

Then there's the "rock house" adjacent to Aliso Creek beach. Literally carved into the rock, from the front you see only a garage door and a curved planted roof. On the beach side, the undulating rock gives way to spacious decks and patios.

And Laguna has its very own castle: Pyne Castle in North Laguna, which was built by Walter E. Pyne over a period of seven years, starting in 1927. Originally a sixty-two-room villa, it's now split into individual apartments, but the original exterior remains.

Keep an eye out for more of Laguna's singular homes: each has its own story.

HISTORIC RESOURCES INVENTORY

Between July 1980 and July 1981, a historic survey was conducted to identify pre-1940 buildings in Laguna Beach that should be protected, provided they met two important criteria. First, the original architecture had to be preserved, and second, the buildings had to represent the character of historic Laguna Beach.

A total of 706 buildings were photographed and recorded for the Historic Resources Inventory, and the list was formally recognized and implemented by the city. More have been added over the years, meaning that Laguna's unique architectural past will live on.

> **who knew?**
>
> Under the terms of California's Mills Act, passed in 1972, property taxes on historically significant buildings can be reduced by as much as 60%.

ARTISTIC MAILBOXES

It's not just one-of-a-kind houses that you'll find in Laguna Beach. Many of the mailboxes outside the homes are equally artistic. Some are abstract and modern, others covered in colorful mosaics, and a few are shaped like animals or aircraft.

There are also mailboxes that are intricate miniature versions of the house they sit in front of, in some cases down to the very angle that the house sits on its lot. See how many unique ones you can spot as you wander around town.

we love...

The mailbox in this illustration belongs to the parish priest's residence adjacent to St. Catherine of Siena Catholic Church.

THE SMALLEST CATHOLIC CHURCH IN THE WORLD

Perched on Park Avenue is one of only a few American Catholic cathedrals in the country. St. Francis-By-The-Sea was constructed in 1933 out of rubble from the Long Beach earthquake. It's now a national landmark, once listed by the Guinness Book of Records as the world's smallest Catholic church.

The building itself measures only seventeen feet by sixty feet, and holds a maximum of forty-eight people for services. Check it out next time you're on Park Avenue, but don't blink, or you'll miss it.

who knew?

The nontraditional décor inside St. Francis-By-The-Sea includes a zodiac beneath the baptistry.

THE MOST BEAUTIFUL (FORMER) SEWAGE TREATMENT PLANT

If you're driving on Broadway passing the Festival of Arts grounds, look up the hill on the opposite side and you'll see something that resembles a lighthouse. So what's a lighthouse doing this far inland? Believe it or not, it's a vent for what was the old sewage treatment plant at the bottom of the hill.

Built in 1932, the plant itself was designed to resemble a small Norman tower, with a Mediterranean influence and an exterior staircase, adding flair to a functional building. When the plant closed, the buildings around the cylinder were demolished, but the tower itself was placed on Laguna Beach's Historic Resources Inventory and will be protected for years to come. It's quite possible that this is the only sewage treatment facility in the country to receive such an honor.

who knew?

The old sewage treatment plant remained open until 1983, when a new one was constructed in Aliso Canyon.

VICTORIA BEACH "PIRATE TOWER"

At the foot of a cliff on Victoria Beach stands a sixty-foot Norman tower with a spired roof, commonly referred to as the Pirate Tower. Built in 1926, it was designed to house a spiral staircase linking the house on Victoria Drive above, known as "La Tour," with the beach below. One of the house's former owners occasionally dressed up as a pirate and hid coins in the gaps and crevices of the tower's concrete exterior, as a treasure hunt for local children, hence the nickname.

Now, the tower is locked and the staircase inaccessible, but it's a landmark of Laguna that, despite its original, practical function, appears more like an abandoned lighthouse ... or maybe someplace that a fairytale heroine may have been imprisoned, staring out to sea as she brushed her long locks of hair.

83

L.E.E.D. PLATINUM HOUSES

Just as Laguna Beach reveres its architectural past, the twenty-first century is also well represented, with innovative architectural designs that not only look good, but benefit the planet. The U.S. Green Building Council's L.E.E.D. program (Leadership in Energy and Environmental Design) awards Platinum status to projects that meet its highest environmental standards. There are currently three houses in Laguna built to meet those standards.

The homes include elements such as solar energy systems, FSC (Forest Stewardship Council) certified wood, low VOC (Volatile Organic Compounds) paints and water reclamation systems. Designed by prominent Laguna Beach architects, the houses are among a very small group of residential properties to be considered for Platinum certification.

SPORTS ON LAND AND SEA

LAGUNA BEACH LAWN BOWLING CLUB

84

SURFING

There are so many ways to enjoy the ocean in Laguna, but surfing is probably the water sport most associated with this community. Laguna Beach holds a special place in the annals of southern California surf history, and Brooks Street Beach is the venue for what's considered to be the longest running surf competition in the country. The Brooks Street Surfing Classic was first held in 1955 and has hosted an impressive list of local legends including Hobie Alter, Bing Boka, Tom Morey, Ron Sizemore, and Corky Carroll. The contest is only open to local surfers, both amateur and professional.

Surf culture continues to be an important part of community life in Laguna Beach. There are a number of surf breaks in town, suited to different levels of ability, and almost every kid learns to surf at some point. Whenever a sizeable swell hits, the pulse of the town picks up noticeably: you'll see kids (and adults!) dashing across Coast Highway toward the beach with surfboards under their arms, in a hurry to get to the waves.

HAKAMA BEACH PALAPA

SEA KAYAKING

Check out the kelp beds, watch the seals at play, and follow a pod of dolphins, all while sitting down. Sea kayaking allows you to get up close and personal with ocean life as you paddle along in either a single or a double craft.

With a partner or a child, you can share the paddling load and head out either on your own or with a group. Kayaking is a great upper body workout, but don't be deceived: your lower half may be seated, but you're still bracing the sides with your legs as you paddle along. Time will fly by as you explore, and the view of the coastline from the water is beautiful to behold.

86

LAWN BOWLING

Like a scene from a bucolic English summer day, white-clad figures slowly stoop to roll gleaming black spheres along the velvety green grass of Heisler Park's bowling green, keeping their eyes on the small white jack in the distance. This is the Laguna Beach Lawn Bowling Club, which has been in operation since 1931. Playing host to the Grand Finals of the U.S. Open of Lawn Bowls, Laguna Beach is a prominent part of the lawn bowling scene.

who knew?

You can also hold private events and corporate meetings at the Lawn Bowling Club.

If you're new to the game and interested to learn, the club offers free introductory lessons to get you acquainted. If you like what you see, you can become a member and even enter tournaments according to your skill level. A very elegant way to spend an afternoon overlooking the ocean.

we love...

The boards used by
professional skimboarders are built using
technology adapted from the aerospace industry to
attain maximum lightness and buoyancy.

SKIMBOARDING

There's one water sport that actually has its origins in Laguna Beach, and that's skimboarding. Lifeguards in the 1920s first used pieces of wood to "skim" the waves, and in the 1970s the sport really took off when Laguna local Charles "Tex" Haines founded Victoria Skimboards. Named after his favorite childhood skimboarding spot, Victoria Beach, Victoria Skimboards was the first company to manufacture and sell skimboards.

Today's boards are a lot more advanced than pieces of carved wood. Modern skimboards are constructed from fiberglass or carbon fiber, with a high-density foam core, and are made to different specifications, depending on the size and skill of the rider. The World Championship of Skimboarding is held every summer in Laguna Beach, attracting the best male and female professional boarders as well as amateurs and children, some as young as five years old.

STAND UP PADDLING

When the ocean is calm and the waves are flat, what's an avid surfer to do? Rather than ride the waves, why not glide across the water instead? In just a few short years, stand up paddling has become one of the hottest water sports in Laguna Beach. Its appeal lies in the fact that you don't have to be a surfer, or a serious athlete of any kind, to have fun. Complete beginners with a decent sense of balance can get the hang of it in no time, skimming the water and watching the dolphins swim by. In warm weather, the ocean is dotted with boards of all shapes and sizes, and there are several companies in town that offer lessons and equipment, both for rent and for sale.

who knew?

Stand up paddling began in the 1960s when surfing instructors needed to position themselves close to their students to take photographs.

SNORKELING AND SCUBA DIVING

If you'd rather be in the water than floating on it, the waters of Laguna Beach are a beautiful place to go snorkeling — or if you're a certified diver, SCUBA diving. Most of Laguna's beaches and coves can be explored underwater, with the most popular being the aptly named Diver's Cove as well as Shaw's Cove, Woods Cove and Crescent Bay.

Keep an eye out for garibaldi, sea cucumbers, starfish and even moray eels. Night diving at Diver's Cove will yield sightings of bat rays, lobsters and horn sharks. Snorkel tours can also be arranged for those who prefer to remain near the surface, and you'll see plenty of ocean life too.

who knew?

The first modern snorkel was devised by Leonardo
da Vinci at the request of the
Venetian senate. It consisted of a
hollow breathing tube that was attached to a
diver's leather helmet.

SKATEBOARDING "GROMS"
ON THE STREETS OF LAGUNA

we love...

The term "grommet," or "grom," refers to a
young participant in extreme sports like surfing,
skimboarding, and skateboarding. Groms tend to
be small in stature but large in spirit.

SKATEBOARDING

With so many steep hills, Laguna Beach has been a mecca for skateboarders for many years. New regulations require all boarders to wear helmets, and since it's possible to get up to speeds of forty miles per hour or more, that's a laudable safety precaution. Popular hills include Nyes Place and Park Avenue. It's important to note that like cyclists, skateboarders share the road with cars, meaning that all parties need to be mindful of each other, and skateboarders must also comply with other road rules, like stopping at stop signs and yielding to traffic. For the most part, everyone pays attention, ensuring that fun and safety can coexist.

MOUNTAIN BIKING

The trails are alive with the sound of ... mountain bikers. Laguna Beach plays host to some of the best mountain bikers in the world who love the variety of trails in and around the wilderness parks. One of the most popular trails is the Rock-It/Cholla Loop, named as one of the one hundred best trails in a guidebook on southern California mountain biking.

The western part of the trail lies in the Laguna Beach Greenbelt, an area of open space that's protected for nature and recreation. Crisscrossing the area above Laguna Canyon Road, most of the trail is designated for intermediate and advanced riders. Mellower trails do exist, along sandy, wide paths, so if you're a beginner, there's something for you too.

BEACH VOLLEYBALL

Laguna's Main Beach is the quintessential family beach, anchored by the iconic lifeguard tower. It offers a kiddie playground, basketball courts, tide pools to explore along Heisler Park, places to picnic, and beach volleyball courts. Volleyball players love the soft sand and the proximity to town. Spectators love to admire the athleticism and skill of the teams as they vie for supremacy. During the busy summer season it can be tough to get in on the action, but come September, it's easier to find an open court. If you've never given beach volleyball a try, Laguna Beach is the perfect spot to begin.

who knew?

Beach volleyball made its first Olympic appearance in 1996.

GOLF

You don't have to leave town if you want to play a round of golf: there's a nine-hole golf course right here at the Ranch at Laguna Beach. Carved into Aliso and Woods Canyons, Ben Brown's golf course has been open since 1950 and the course works with the natural landscape formations, offering challenges for all players. As the golfers swing through, a variety of canyon wildlife also goes about its business. There's even a family of deer living among the rocks and bushes.

When you're done with the nine, take a load off at the proverbial "tenth hole." The on-site restaurant has a patio that overlooks the course. Even if you're not a golfer, it's a beautiful place to relax and enjoy the scenery.

FAMOUS PLACES AND FACES

BETTE DAVIS'S HOUSE

94

MOVIE-MAKING

Some of Laguna's picturesque beaches and coves resemble deserted islands, and that's exactly why they've been used as movie sets. Treasure Island Beach is aptly named for one of the most famous movies, when scenes from *Treasure Island* were shot there in 1939. But the beach was a popular location prior to that, when parts of the 1920 movie *The Adventures of Robinson Crusoe* and other features from the 1920s were filmed there.

In 1942, scenes from *Now, Voyager*, starring Bette Davis, were shot at the Victor Hugo Inn, now Las Brisas Restaurant. In 1954, parts of the Judy Garland classic, *A Star is Born*, were also shot in town. More recently, Laguna Beach was featured in scenes from 1992's *A Few Good Men* and Oliver Stone's 2012 movie, *Savages*. Hollywood's love affair with Laguna Beach continues.

ICONIC RESIDENCES

When Laguna Beach became a favored place to shoot movies in the first half of the twentieth century, many actors and producers fell in love with the town and purchased homes here to escape the bustle of Hollywood.

Maybe the most famous residence is Bette Davis's former house in Woods Cove: an English Tudor-style home, built in 1929, with its signature "D" on the chimneystack. Davis lived in the house during the 1940s and although she resided in many other places before her death, she once referred to her Laguna Beach house during an interview with Johnny Carson, saying it was her favorite, and that she still thought of it as home.

we love...

Another iconic Laguna Beach residence, the Proctor House in Three Arch Bay, was built in 1933 by General H.N. Proctor and is an exact copy of a French home in which he was billeted during the First World War.

ATHLETES, OLYMPIANS AND MORE

In addition to the artistic members of the community, explorers, athletes and other luminaries have also called Laguna Beach home. These include Richard Halliburton, the adventurer, who built another of Laguna's iconic homes, dubbed the "hangover house;" pioneer aviatrix Florence "Pancho" Barnes; and the infamous Timothy Leary.

Today, there are many world-class athletes, including Olympians, who live in town, as well as bright stars from the worlds of finance, music, business, medicine, and even space.

who knew?

Bette Davis's mother also lived in Laguna Beach. She died here in 1960.

ACTORS, ARTISTS, MUSICIANS AND WRITERS

The list of well-known people who chose to make Laguna their home is long, and the town continues to be a draw for people from many artistic disciplines. While the privacy of current residents is a priority, here are a few former famous residents of Laguna Beach.

Actors Mary Pickford, Douglas Fairbanks, Charlie Chaplin, Mickey Rooney, Rudolph Valentino, Judy Garland and Bette Davis. Writer John Steinbeck, who wrote his famed book *Tortilla Flat* while living on Park Avenue. Songwriter Jack Norworth, who wrote the ubiquitous summer ditty, *Take Me Out To The Ballgame*. And, of course, there were painters, including Frank Cuprien and William Wendt, who was known as the "Dean of Southern California Artists."

MENTON, FRANCE

SISTER CITIES

The comparisons between Laguna Beach and the French Riviera are plentiful, so it makes sense that the town's first official sister city, chosen in 2008, is Menton, on the Cote D'Azur in France. Like Laguna Beach, Menton has around 25,000 residents and a large population of tourists flocking to its beaches and festivals.

San Jose Del Cabo in Mexico is Laguna's second sister city. Situated at the tip of the Baja Peninsula, it too is a major tourist destination, with white sandy beaches and upscale resorts. The town even has a First Thursday Art Walk every month, as Laguna does.

St. Ives, a small seaside town on the south coast of England is Laguna Beach's newest sister city. Just like Laguna, St. Ives has a thriving artistic community, great waves for surfing and an economy based on tourism.

we love...

St. Ives was granted its charter by King Edward I in 1295 — the town is almost 800 years old!

JOHN WAYNE AIRPORT

What's not to love about a local airport named for one of the biggest names in movies? And it has a statue of the man, to boot. Ah, but it's not in Laguna Beach, you say. And yes, that's true, but something about this airport affects everyone in town. You see, there's a curfew, and that's great for all of us.

There are no takeoffs before 7 a.m. during the week (8 a.m. on Sundays), and no landings after 10:30 p.m. What that means for Laguna Beach is quiet nights and peaceful mornings. There are no jet engines to disrupt our beauty sleep, and for many locals, John Wayne airport provides a morning alarm of sorts. You always know it's just past 7 a.m. when the first planes start to fly over.

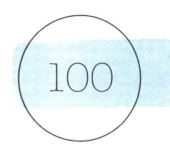

100

FAMOUS DOGS

There are four-legged superstars living in Laguna Beach as well as two-legged ones. The Westminster Dog Show is the nation's oldest and most prestigious canine event, and Laguna can boast that it's home to a couple of the best dogs in the business, having placed first in their breed at Westminster. One of them was recently even first in his group, competing for the final prize: Best In Show. While they may have fancy names when they compete in the show ring, when they're at home, these dogs live their own versions of the Laguna Beach lifestyle, jogging on the beach and hanging out with their people. All in a day's work.

who knew?

Dogs on leashes are allowed on Laguna's beaches any time between September 11 and June 14. During the busy summer months, access is restricted to before 9 a.m. and after 6 p.m.

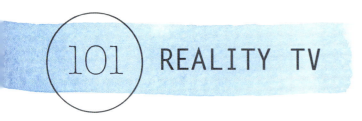

101 REALITY TV

THE ONE WE LOVE TO HATE, AND HATE TO LOVE

Perception of Laguna Beach — and Orange County in general — can arguably be divided into pre- and post-reality TV eras. Prior to 2004, the town was on the map for many of the reasons in this book, and a lot more. But for those who didn't know much about the city, describing its location went along the lines of "midway between L.A. and San Diego." After the cameras descended, Laguna Beach was firmly established in pop culture, bringing many more visitors, and worldwide recognition.

THE REAL LAGUNA BEACH

And that's the double-edged sword. Laguna locals understand what's "real" and what's not, and don't always recognize or value the version of their community that they see on TV. The influx of visitors interested in these shows has been a boon for business, but we really want people to love Laguna for the right reasons.

With or without the TV cameras, Laguna Beach will continue to change and grow, while preserving its heritage. Geography and topography dictate that its rugged beauty and compact character will remain intact, and years from now, it will still be recognizable as the place it has been for generations. While pop culture will move on to the next big thing, Laguna Beach will always be what it is today: a coastal haven for residents, visitors, nature and wildlife.

ABOUT
THE AUTHORS

HELEN POLINS-JONES [ILLUSTRATOR]

British-born watercolor artist Helen Polins-Jones lives and works in Laguna Beach. Using pencil and watercolor, she creates illustrations, motifs and patterns that can be found on a variety of handmade products in local gift stores. Helen's favorite item on the list is the sea birds, which she loves to watch in action while walking along the beach.

SALLY EASTWOOD [AUTHOR]

British native Sally Eastwood has lived in Laguna Beach since 2000, after eight years on the Eastern Seaboard. During her corporate life, Sally has written presentations, speeches, scripts and more, and now writes from her home with a view of the ocean and her dogs at her feet. Sally's favorite item on the list is Laguna's goats, the four-legged firefighters who spend all day eating on the job.

ACKNOWLEDGMENTS

Thanks to Mary Hurlbut for the photographs on pages 27, 31, 33, 49, 52, 62-63, 79, 81, 86-88, 95, 99, 101, 104-105, 106, 127, 142, and 145. For more information about Mary and her work, visit www.maryhurlbutphoto.com.

Thanks to Cathleen Falsani Possley for the photograph on page 53.

Thanks to Lisa Aslanian of the George Gallery and Carla Tesak Arzente of Salt Fine Art for the photographs on page 65.

Thanks to Baldemar Fierro for the image of Andrew Myers's "The Shopper" statue on page 67.

Thanks to Lisa Burchi for her photograph on page 83.

Thanks to Horst Noppenberger for the photographs on page 121.

Thanks to Corinne Conklin for her photographs on page 136.

Thanks to Carmen Freeman Rey for her photograph (lower right) on Page 145.

Historic photographs on pages 13, 17 and 107 courtesy of the Laguna Beach Historical Society.

Photographs on page 60 courtesy of Laguna Beach Festival of Arts.

Photographs of the authors courtesy of April Brian.

All other photographs courtesy of the authors and Brooks Street Books.

RESOURCES

The authors would like to acknowledge the following publications and websites for the wealth of factual information included in this book:

- *The Cottages and Castles of Laguna: Historic Architecture 1883-1940* by Karen Wilson Turnbull, 1987.
- *Laguna Beach, California*, An Illustrated Narrative History by Roger W. Jones, 2003.
- *The First 100 Years in Laguna Beach 1876-1976* by Merle and Mabel Ramsey, 1976.
- *Visit Laguna Beach – the Official Visitors' Center:* www.visitlagunabeach.com
- Steve Turnbull's website: www.light-headed.com
- The websites of many of the institutions mentioned in the book

www.brooksstreetbooks.com